Selected Poems

GILLIAN CLARKE

Selected Poems

For David Thomas

First published in 1985 by
Carcanet Press Limited
208-212 Corn Exchange Buildings
Manchester M4 3BQ

British Library Cataloguing in Publication Data
Clarke, Gillian
    Selected poems.
    I. Title
    821'.914   PR6053.L328
    ISBN 0-85635-594-1

The publisher acknowledges the financial assistance
of the Arts Council of Great Britain.

Typeset by Bryan Williamson, Swinton, Berwickshire
Printed in England by SRP Ltd, Exeter

Contents

New Poems

The Sundial

Owain was ill today. In the night
He was delirious, shouting of lions
In the sleepless heat. Today, dry
And pale, he took a paper circle,
Laid it on the grass which held it
With curling fingers. In the still
Centre he pushed the broken bean
Stick, gathering twelve fragments
Of stone, placed them at measured
Distances. Then he crouched, slightly
Trembling with fever, calculating
The mathematics of sunshine.

He looked up, his eyes dark,
Intelligently adult as though
The wave of fever taught silence
And immobility for the first time.
Here, in his enforced rest, he found
Deliberation, and the slow finger
Of light, quieter than night lions,
More worthy of his concentration.
All day he told the time to me.
All day we felt and watched the sun
Caged in its white diurnal heat,
Pointing at us with its black stick.

Journey

As far as I am concerned
We are driving into oblivion.
On either side there is nothing,
And beyond your driving
Shaft of light it is black.
You are a miner digging
For a future, a mineral
Relationship in the dark.
I can hear the darkness drip
From the other world where people
Might be sleeping, might be alive.

Certainly there are white
Gates with churns waiting
For morning, their cream standing.
Once we saw an old table
Standing square on the grass verge.
Our lamps swept it clean, shook
The crumbs into the hedge and left it.
A tractor too, beside a load
Of logs, bringing from a deeper
Dark a damp whiff of the fungoid
Sterility of the conifers.

Complacently I sit, swathed
In sleepiness. A door shuts
At the end of a dark corridor.
Ahead not a cat's eye winks
To deceive us with its green
Invitation. As you hurl us
Into the black contracting
Chasm, I submit like a blind
And folded baby, being born.

Snow on the Mountain

There was a girl riding a white pony
Which seemed an elemental part
Of the snow. A crow cut a clean line
Across the hill, which we grasped as a rope
To pull us up the pale diagonal.

The point was to be first at the top
Of the mountain. Our laughter bounced far
Below us like five fists full of pebbles. About us
Lay the snow, deep in the hollows,
Very clean and dry, untouched.

I arrived breathless, my head breaking
The surface of the glittering light, thinking
No place could claim more beauty, white
Slag tips like cones of sugar spun
By the pit wheels under Machen mountain.

I sat on a rock in the sun, watching
My snowboys play. Pit villages shine
Like anthracite. Completed, the pale rider
Rode away. I turned to him and saw
His joy fall like the laughter down a dark
Crack. The black crow shadowed him.

Blaen Cwrt

You ask how it is. I will tell you.
There is no glass. The air spins in
The stone rectangle. We warm our hands
With apple wood. Some of the smoke
Rises against the ploughed, brown field
As a sign to our neighbours in the
Four folds of the valley that we are in.
Some of the smoke seeps through the stones
Into the barn where it curls like fern
On the walls. Holding a thick root
I press my bucket through the surface
Of the water, lift it brimming and skim
The leaves away. Our fingers curl on
Enamel mugs of tea, like ploughmen.
The stones clear in the rain
Giving their colours. It's not easy.
There are no brochure blues or boiled sweet
Reds. All is ochre and earth and cloud-green
Nettles tasting sour and the smells of moist
Earth and sheep's wool. The wattle and daub
Chimney hood has decayed away, slowly
Creeping to dust, chalking the slate
Floor with stories. It has all the first
Necessities for a high standard
Of civilised living: silence inside
A circle of sound, water and fire,
Light on uncountable miles of mountain
From a big, unpredictable sky,
Two rooms, waking and sleeping,
Two languages, two centuries of past
To ponder on, and the basic need
To work hard in order to survive.

Baby-Sitting

I am sitting in a strange room listening
For the wrong baby. I don't love
This baby. She is sleeping a snuffly
Roseate, bubbling sleep; she is fair;
She is a perfectly acceptable child.
I am afraid of her. If she wakes
She will hate me. She will shout
Her hot midnight rage, her nose
Will stream disgustingly and the perfume
Of her breath will fail to enchant me.

To her I will represent absolute
Abandonment. For her it will be worse
Than for the lover cold in lonely
Sheets; worse than for the woman who waits
A moment to collect her dignity
Beside the bleached bone in the terminal ward.
As she rises sobbing from the monstrous land
Stretching for milk-familiar comforting,
She will find me and between us two
It will not come. It will not come.

Birth

On the hottest, stillest day of the summer
A calf was born in a field
At Pant-y-Cetris; two buzzards
Measured the volume of the sky;
The hills brimmed with incoming
Night. In the long grass we could see
The cow, her sides heaving, a focus
Of restlessness in the complete calm,
Her calling at odds with silence.

The light flowed out leaving stars
And clarity. Hot and slippery, the scalding
Baby came, and the cow stood up, her cool
Flanks like white flowers in the dark.
We waited while the calf struggled
To stand, moved as though this
Were the first time. I could feel the soft sucking
Of the new-born, the tugging pleasure
Of bruised reordering, the signal
Of milk's incoming tide, and satisfaction
Fall like a clean sheet around us.

Nightride

The road unwinding under our wheels
New in the headlamps like a roll of foil.
The rain is a recorder writing tunes
In telegraph wires, kerbs and cats' eyes,
Reflections and the lights of little towns.

He turns his head to look at me.
"Why are you quiet?" Shiny road rhythm,
Rain rhythm, beat of the windscreen wipers,
I push my knee against his in the warmth
And the car thrusts the dark and rain away.

The child sleeps, and I reflect, as I breathe
His brown hair, and watch the apple they gave him
Held in his hot hands, that a tree must ache
With the sweet weight of the round rosy fruit,
As I with Dylan's head, nodding on its stalk.

Catrin

I can remember you, child,
As I stood in a hot, white
Room at the window watching
The people and cars taking
Turn at the traffic lights.
I can remember you, our first
Fierce confrontation, the tight
Red rope of love which we both
Fought over. It was a square
Environmental blank, disinfected
Of paintings or toys. I wrote
All over the walls with my
Words, coloured the clean squares
With the wild, tender circles
Of our struggle to become
Separate. We want, we shouted,
To be two, to be ourselves.

Neither won nor lost the struggle
In the glass tank clouded with feelings
Which changed us both. Still I am fighting
You off, as you stand there
With your straight, strong, long
Brown hair and your rosy,
Defiant glare, bringing up
From the heart's pool that old rope,
Tightening about my life,
Trailing love and conflict,
As you ask may you skate
In the dark, for one more hour.

Still Life

It was good tonight
To polish brass with you,
Our hands slightly gritty
With Brasso, as they would feel
If we'd been in the sea, salty.
It was as if we burnished
Our friendship, polished it
Until all the light-drowning
Tarnish of deceit
Were stroked away. Patterns
Of incredible honesty
Delicately grew, revealed
Quite openly to the pressure
Of the soft, torn rag.
We made a yellow-gold
Still-life out of clocks,
Candlesticks and kettles.
My sadness puzzled you.
I rubbed the full curve
Of an Indian goblet,
Feeling its illusory
Heat. It cooled beneath
My fingers and I read
In the braille formality
Of pattern, in the leaf
And tendril and stylised tree,
That essentially each
Object remains cold,
Separate, only reflecting
The other's warmth.

Storm Awst

The cat walks. It listens, as I do,
To the wind which leans its iron
Shoulders on our door. Neither
The purr of a cat nor my blood
Runs smoothly for elemental fear
Of the storm. This then is the big weather
They said was coming. All the signs
Were bad, the gulls coming in white,
Lapwings gathering, the sheep too
Calling all night. The gypsies
Were making their fires in the woods
Down there in the east. . .always
A warning. The rain stings, the whips
Of the laburnum hedge lash the roof
Of the cringing cottage. A curious
Calm, coming from the storm, unites
Us, as we wonder if the work
We have done will stand. Will the tyddyn,
In its group of strong trees on the high
Hill, hold against the storm Awst
Running across hills where everything
Alive listens, pacing its house, heart still?

Death of a Young Woman

She died on a hot day. In a way
Nothing was different. The stretched white
Sheet of her skin tightened no further.
She was fragile as a yacht before,
Floating so still on the blue day's length,
That one would not know when the breath
Blew out and the sail finally slackened.
Her eyes had looked opaquely in the
Wrong place to find those who smiled
From the bedside, and for a long time
Our conversations were silent.

The difference was that in her house
The people were broken by her loss.
He wept for her and for the hard tasks
He had lovingly done, for the short,
Fierce life she had lived in the white bed,
For the burden he had put down for good.
As we sat huddled in pubs supporting
Him with beer and words' warm breath,
We felt the hollowness of his release.
Our own ungrateful health prowled, young,
Gauche about her death. He was polite,
Isolated. Free. No point in going home.

Swinging

At the end of the hot day it rains
Softly, stirring the smells from the raked
Soil. In her sundress and shorts she rocks
On the swing, watching the rain run down
Her brown arms, hands folded warm between
Small thighs, watching her white daps darken
And soak in the cut and sodden grass.

She used to fling her anguish into
My arms, staining my solitude with
Her salt and grimy griefs. Older now
She runs, her violence prevailing
Against silence and the avenue's
Complacency, I her hatred's object.

Her dress, the washed green of deck chairs, sun
Bleached and chalk-sea rinsed, colours the drops,
And her hair a flag, half and then full
Mast in the apple-trees, flies in the face
Of the rain. Raised now her hands grip tight
The iron rods, her legs thrusting the tide
Of rain aside until, parallel
With the sky, she triumphs and gently
Falls. A green kite. I wind in the string.

Waterfall

We parked the car in a dusty village
That sat sideways on a hill over the coal.
We heard a rag-and-bone man
And a curlew. The sun for the first time
Put a warm hand across our shoulders
And touched our winter faces.

We saw summer, one lapwing to go,
Her mate was in the sky already,
Turning over, black, white-bellied,
While she, looking browner near the ground,
Tidied the winter from her crisp field.

We climbed the mountain, crossed the round
Of it, following the marshland down to the gorge.
The water was gathering minutely everywhere
Knowing its place and its time were coming.

Down over the boulders in the death bed
Of an old river, through thin birches and oaks,
Going where the water went, into the multitude
Of the shouting streams, no longer speaking
To each other, silenced by what the water said.

Closer to crisis the air put cold silk
Against our faces and the cliffs streamed
With sun water, caging on every gilded
Ledge small things that flew by mistake
Into the dark spaces behind the rainbows.

The path led me under the fall to feel
The arc of the river and the mountain's exact
Weight; the roar of rain and lapwings
Leaving; water-beat, heart-fall in accord,
Curlew-call, child-cry on the drum's skin
Distinguished from the inmost thoughts of rivers.

We cage our response in the roar, defer
Decision while water falls. It gathers its life
On our behalf, leaps for us, its chords
Of change that curve across the cliffs
Are only, after all, an altering of level
To where it belongs, though the falling appals.

Lunchtime Lecture

And this from the second or third millenium
B.C., a female, aged about twenty-two.
A white, fine skull, full up with darkness
As a shell with sea, drowned in the centuries.
Small, perfect. The cranium would fit the palm
Of a man's hand. Some plague or violence
Destroyed her, and her whiteness lay safe in a shroud
Of silence, undisturbed, unrained on, dark
For four thousand years. Till a tractor in summer
Biting its way through the longcairn for supplies
Of stone, broke open the grave and let a crowd of light
Stare in at her, and she stared quietly back.

As I look at her I feel none of the shock
The farmer felt as, unprepared, he found her.
Here in the Museum, like death in hospital,
Reasons are given, labels, causes, catalogues.
The smell of death is done. Left, only her bone
Purity, the light and shade beauty that her man
Was denied sight of, the perfect edge of the place
Where the pieces join, with no mistakes, like boundaries.

She's a tree in winter, stripped white on a black sky,
Leafless formality, brow, bough in fine relief.
I, at some other season, illustrate the tree
Fleshed, with woman's hair and colours and the rustling
Blood, the troubled mind that she has overthrown.
We stare at each other, dark into sightless
Dark, seeing only ourselves in the black pools,
Gulping the risen sea that booms in the shell.

Dyddgu Replies to Dafydd

All year in open places, underneath
    the frescoed forest ceiling,
    we have made ceremony
    out of this seasonal love.

Dividing the leaf-shade as divers white
    in green pools we rose to dry
    islands of sudden sun. Then
    love seemed generosity.

Original sin I whitened from your
    mind, my colours influenced
    your flesh, as sun on the floor
    and warm furniture of a church.

So did our season bloom in mild weather,
    reflected gold like butter
    under chins, repeatedly
    unfolding to its clock of seed.

Autumn, our forest room is growing cold.
    I wait, shivering, feeling a
    dropping sun, a coming dark,
    your heart changing the subject.

The season coughs as it falls, like a coal;
    the trees ache. The forest falls
    to ruin, a roofless minster
    where only two still worship.

Love still, like sun, a vestment, celebrates,
    its warmth about our shoulders.
    I dread the day when Dyddgu's once
    loved name becomes a common cloak.

Your touch is not so light. I grow heavy.
    I wait too long, grow anxious,
    note your changing gestures, fear
    desire's alteration.

The winter stars are flying and the owls
    sing. You are packing your songs
    in a sack, narrowing your
    words, as you stare at the road.

The feet of young men beat, somewhere far off
    on the mountain. I would women
    had roads to tread in winter
    and other lovers waiting.

A raging rose all summer falls to snow,
    keeps its continuance in
    frozen soil. I must be patient
    for the breaking of the crust.

I must be patient that you will return
    when the wind whitens the tender
    underbelly of the March grass
    thick as pillows under the oaks.

At Ystrad Fflûr

No way of flowers at this late season.
  Only a river blossoming on stone
  and the mountain ash in fruit.

All rivers are young in these wooded hills
  where the abbey watches and the young Teifi
  counts her rosary on stones.

I cross by a simple bridge constructed
  of three slim trees. Two lie across. The third
  is a broken balustrade.

The sun is warm after rain on the red
  pelt of the slope, fragmentary through trees
  like torches in the dark.

They have been here before me and have seen
  the sun's lunulae in the profound
  quietness of water.

The Teifi is in full flood and rich
  with metals: a torc in a brown pool
  gleaming for centuries.

I am spellbound in a place of spells. Cloud
  changes gold to stone as their circled bones
  dissolve in risen corn.

The river races for the south too full
  of summer rain for safety, spilt water
  whitening low-lying fields.

From oak and birchwoods through the turning trees
  where leaf and hour and century fall
  seasonally, desire runs

Like sparks in stubble through the memory
  of the place, and a yellow mustard field
  is a sheet of flame in the heart.

Sheep's Skulls

The bone is thin as paper
Inside the skull, scrolled on shadow.
Its dreams evaporated
On a warm bank over the drover's road
To Capel Cynon.

We sought skulls like mushrooms,
Uncertainly white at a distance,
Skulls of sheep, rabbit, bird,
Beautiful as a leaf's skeleton
Or derelict shell,

Where sheep shelter inside stone
Cottages, graze the floors clean, stare
From the window spaces. They die
On the open hill, and raven and buzzard
Come like women to clean them.

The skull's caves are secretive.
The crazed bone, sometimes translucent
As vellum, sometimes shawled
To lace, no longer knocks with the heart's bell
To the lamb in the womb.

A spider wraps it in a tress
Of silk, a cloth of light. On the rose
Patina of old wood it lies
Ornamental in the reflection
Of a jar of wheat stalks.

Railway Tracks

When you talk to me of carrots fresh pulled
From your grandfather's allotment, how he
Would wash the soil away in the green rain
Of the water butt, and then shake them dry;
When I see you carry your fruit away
To the railway bank, and feast there neck high
In golden, seeded grass and flowering weeds,
I see my own mysterious railway track,
Ragwort, dog daisies and valerian
Swim in the great heat on the waves of grass.
Sweet surreptitious smells, like tar and sweat,
And dusty arms, and pollen on my knees.
A vast, dead brick building with a hundred
Broken windows, the track losing its way
Besieged by leaf and stalk and flowerhead
Triumphant to be brought again to their
Own country. Above all, leaping from sleeper
To sleeper, along these lines that lead deep
And parallel into the wilderness,
I hear another footfall follow mine.

But who that child was, what the happiness,
And where the track, no one can tell me now.
It was as good as carrots on the bank
To find a place where wildness had returned.
The old, blind warehouse, full of swooping birds,
Has given me a taste for dereliction,
For the fall of towers, the rot of stone and brick,
For the riot of the ragged weed's return,
The reinstatement of the wilderness.

In Pisgah Graveyard

Dylan tells me this is a church-garden.
Indeed, these bones, ground seed-small, seem neither
Static nor dead. The flowers that flourish
Here suggest fertility, the seed-heads
Of late summer brave, casting away
Their foliage, the naked sky. *Er côf*
On every stone, I count the time each
One was allowed, arrange their families,
Imagined, in the old farms and places
That watch still from the mountains.

The warmth tumbles here like a giant sun
Flower dying and full of glossy seed.
This roughest stone of all, a sand-stone pod
Bursting with words, is Dewi Emrys's grave.
And all around the living corn concedes
Fecundity to him. They're proud of him
Here, where full barns count as much as poetry.
He who, they say, knew women as well as words,
Lies in the blond fields blowing to seed
With the threshing machine and the chapel clock.

What do I look for here, with a child's
Hot hand in mine, his hair like ragged robin?
Perhaps the stone words of my first tongue
On a poet's grave that tidies his wild life,
For the savage roar of the trapped sun
Seeding the earth against the stop of winter
When everything that lives will play dead lions,
And the flaming mane of the surrounding wheat
Drops down, lies still until, inside the heart,
The words unfreeze and the poems come again.

Foghorns

When Catrin was a small child
She thought the foghorn moaning
Far out at sea was the sad
Solitary voice of the moon
Journeying to England.
She heard it warn "Moon, Moon",
As it worked the Channel, trading
Weather like rags and bones.

Tonight, after the still sun
And the silent heat, as haze
Became rain and weighed glistening
In brimful leaves, and the last bus
Splashes and fades with a soft
Wave-sound, the foghorns moan, moon-
Lonely and the dry lawns drink.
This dimmed moon, calling still,
Hauls sea-rags through the streets.

Curlew

She dips her bill in the rim of the sea.
Her beak is the ellipse
of a world much smaller
than that far section of the sea's
circumference. A curve enough to calculate
the field's circle and its heart
of eggs in the cold grass.

All day while I scythed my territory
out of nettles, laid claim to my cantref,
she has cut her share of sky. Her song bubbles
long as a plane trail from her savage mouth.
I clean the blade with newspaper. Dusk blurs
circle within circle till there's nothing left
but the egg pulsing in the dark against her ribs.
For each of us the possessed space contracts
to the nest's heat, the blood's small circuit.

St Augustine's, Penarth

The church is like the prow
Of a smoky ship, moving
On the down channel currents
To the open sea. A stone

Figurehead, the flowing light
Streams from it. From everywhere
You can see Top Church, remote
As high church is from chapel.

Church high on the summit
Of the climbing town
Where I was a child, where rain
Runs always slantingly

On streets like tilted chutes
Of grey sliding on all sides
From the church, to sea and dock,
To shopping streets and home.

Breasting the cloud, its stone
Profile of an ancient priest
Preaches continuity
In the face of turning tides.

Burning Nettles

Where water springs, pools, waits
Collection in a bucket
In the late summer heat,
Beech trees observe foresight
Of autumn wrinkling their leaves.
The cold will wither this
Old garden. The plumpness shrinks
Beneath its skin, a light
Frown puckers the mirrored sky.

The scythe bleeds ancient herbs
Whose odours come as ghosts
To disturb memory.
My fire of nettles crackles
Like bees creeping in a green
Hive, making white smoke from weeds,
And the strange, sweet plants Marged
Sowed, or Nanu, before
The wind changed from the east.

With the reaping hook blade
I lift an exhausted moth
From the hot mound. It lives
To die of cold. Inside the cave
Of thatched grass the secret fire
Thrives on my summer. Nettles
Turn to ashes in its heart,
Crucible of the fragrant and
The sour. Only soil survives.

Rose bay willowherb, ragwort,
Grass, disintegrate and make
A white continuous mane
For the mountain. Ponies turn
Windward. The evening's heat
Belies the beech tree's shiver,

And pinpoints of ice on skin
Are nettlestings, not rain. Fire,
Buried in flower-heads, makes
Bright ritual of decay,
Transubstantiates the green
Leaf to fertility.

Last Rites

During this summer of the long drought
The road to Synod Inn has kept
Its stigmata of dust and barley seed;

At the inquest they tell it again:
How the lorry tents us from the sun,
His pulse dangerous in my hands,
A mains hum only, no message
Coming through. His face warm, profiled
Against tarmac, the two-stroke Yamaha
Dead as a black horse in a war.
Only his hair moves and the sound
Of the parched grass and harebells a handspan
Away, his fear still with me like the scream
Of a jet in an empty sky.
I cover him with the grey blanket
From my bed, touch his face as a child
Who makes her favourites cosy.
His blood on my hands, his cariad in my arms.

Driving her home we share that vision
Over August fields dying of drought
Of the summer seas shattering
At every turn of Cardigan Bay
Under the cruel stones of the sun.

Harvest at Mynachlog

At last the women come with baskets,
The older one in flowered apron,
A daisied cloth covering the bread
And dappled china, sweet tea
In a vast can. The women stoop
Spreading their cups in the clover.

The engines stop. A buzzard watches
From the fence. We bury our wounds
In the deep grass: sunburnt shoulders,
Bodies scratched with straw, wrists bruised
From the weight of the bales, blood beating.

For hours the baler has been moulding
Golden bricks from the spread straw,
Spewing them at random in the stubble.
I followed the slow load, heaved each
Hot burden, feeling the sun contained.

And unseen over me a man leaned,
Taking the weight to make the toppling
Load. Then the women came, friendly
And cool as patches of flowers at the far
Field edge, mothy and blurred in the heat.

We are soon recovered and roll over
In the grass to take our tea. We talk
Of other harvests. They remember
How a boy, flying his plane so low
Over the cut fields that his father

Straightened from his work to wave his hat
At the boasting sky, died minutes later
On an English cliff, in such a year
As this, the barns brimming gold.

We are quiet again, holding our cups
In turn for the tilting milk, sad, hearing
The sun roar like a rush of grain
Engulfing all winged things that live
One moment in the eclipsing light.

Clywedog

The people came out in pairs,
Old, most of them, holding their places
Close till the very last minute,
Even planting the beans as usual
That year, grown at last accustomed
To the pulse of the bulldozers.
High in those uphill gardens, scarlet
Beanflowers blazed hours after
The water rose in the throats of the farms.

Only the rooted things stayed:
The wasted hay, the drowned
Dog roses, the farms, their kitchens silted
With their own stones, hedges
And walls a thousand years old.
And the mountains, in a head-collar
Of flood, observe a desolation
They'd grown used to before the coming
Of the wall-makers. Language
Crumbles to wind and bird-call.

Choughs

I follow you downhill to the edge
My feet taking as naturally as yours
To a sideways tread, finding footholds
Easily in the turf, accustomed
As we are to a sloping country.

The cliffs buttress the bay's curve to the north
And here drop sheer and sudden to the sea.
The choughs plummet from sight then ride
The updraught of the cliffs' mild yellow
Light, fold, fall with closed wings from the sky.

At the last moment as in unison they turn
A ripcord of the wind is pulled in time.
He gives her food and the saliva
Of his red mouth, draws her black feathers, sweet
As shining grass across his bill.

Rare birds that pair for life. There they go
Divebombing the marbled wave a yard
Above the spray. Wings flick open
A stoop away
From the drawn teeth of the sea.

St Thomas's Day

It's the darkest morning of the year.
Day breaks in water runnels
In the yard: a flutter
Of light on a tiled roof;
The loosening of night's
Stonehold on tap and bolt.

Rain on my face wakes me
From recent sleep. I cross
The yard, shovel bumping
In the barrow, fingers
Stiff as hinges. Catrin
Brings bran and fresh hay.

A snort in the dark, a shove
For supremacy.
My hands are warmed
In the steam of his welcome.
Midwinter, only here
Do the fields still summer,
Thistlehead and flower
Powdered by hoof and tooth.

White Roses

Outside the green velvet sitting room
white roses bloom after rain.
They hold water and sunlight
like cups of fine white china.

Within the boy who sleeps in my care
in the big chair the cold bloom
opens at terrible speed
and the splinter of ice moves

in his blood as he stirs in the chair.
Remembering me he smiles
politely, gritting his teeth
in silence on pain's red blaze.

A stick man in the ashes, his fires
die back. He is spars and springs.
He can talk again, gather
his cat to his bones. She springs

with a small cry in her throat, kneading
with diamond paws his dry
as tinder flesh. The least spark
of pain will burn him like straw.

The sun carelessly shines after rain.
The cat tracks thrushes in sweet
dark soil. And without concern
the rose outlives the child.

Login

Chapel and bridge. A headlong fall
into woods. A river running fast
divides the wild cow parsley.
"My father lived here once," I said,
"I think you knew him."

The sun, hot at our backs, whitens
the lane. She, in shadow, allows
the sun to pass her into the passage.
I gain entry at his name, tea,
a lace cloth on the table.

When talking is done she ruffles
my son's brown hair with a hand
that is bruised with age. Veins stand,
fast water in her wrists. Handshakes,
glances converging could not span
such giddy water.

Out in the lane the thrush outsings
the river. The village is at lunch.
The bridge burns with cow parsley.
We stand in the brilliance without words,
watch him running into the light.

Should he turn now to wave and wait
for me, where sunlight concentrates
blindingly on the bridge, he'd see
all this in sepia, hear footsteps
not yet taken fade away.

Miracle on St David's Day

> "They flash upon that inward eye
> Which is the bliss of solitude"
> *The Daffodils by W. Wordsworth*

An afternoon yellow and open-mouthed
with daffodils. The sun treads the path
among cedars and enormous oaks.
It might be a country house, guests strolling,
the rumps of gardeners between nursery shrubs.

I am reading poetry to the insane.
An old woman, interrupting, offers
as many buckets of coal as I need.
A beautiful chestnut-haired boy listens
entirely absorbed. A schizophrenic

on a good day, they tell me later.
In a cage of first March sun a woman
sits not listening, not seeing, not feeling.
In her neat clothes the woman is absent.
A big, mild man is tenderly led

to his chair. He has never spoken.
His labourer's hands on his knees, he rocks
gently to the rhythms of the poems.
I read to their presences, absences,
to the big, dumb labouring man as he rocks.

He is suddenly standing, silently,
huge and mild, but I feel afraid. Like slow
movement of spring water or the first bird
of the year in the breaking darkness,
the labourer's voice recites "The Daffodils".

The nurses are frozen, alert; the patients
seem to listen. He is hoarse but word-perfect.
Outside the daffodils are still as wax,
a thousand, ten thousand, their syllables
unspoken, their creams and yellows still.

Forty years ago, in a Valleys school,
the class recited poetry by rote.
Since the dumbness of misery fell
he has remembered there was a music
of speech and that once he had something to say.

When he's done, before the applause, we observe
the flowers' silence. A thrush sings
and the daffodils are flame.

Chalk Pebble

The heels of the foetus knead
the stone's roundness out of shape,
downtreading flesh, distorting
the ellipses of the sphere.

It is unexpectedly
salty to touch, its texture
warmer, rougher, weightier
in my hand than I had thought.

Boisterous in its bone
cradle, a stone-breaker,
thief in its mother's orchard,
it is apple-round.

Here the navel
knots it from its chalk down;
there the pressure as the embryo
kicks against ribcage and hip.

The cicatrice of a flower
is printed on one of its
curved surfaces. I carry it
as I walk Glamorgan beaches,

a warm, strange thing to worry
with my fingers. The fossil locked
in its belly stirs, a tender
fresh upheaval of the stone.

East Moors

At the end of a bitter April
the cherries flower at last in Penylan.
We notice the white trees and the flash
of sea with two blue islands beyond
the city, where the steelworks used to smoke.

I live in the house I was born in,
am accustomed to the sudden glow
of flame in the night sky, the dark sound
of something heavy dropped, miles off,
the smell of sulphur almost natural.

In Roath and Rumney now, washing strung
down the narrow gardens will stay clean.
Lethargy settles in front rooms and wives
have lined up little jobs for men to do.
At East Moors they closed the steelworks down.

A few men stay to see it through. Theirs
the bitterest time as rolling mills
make rubble. Demolition gangs
erase skylines whose hieroglyphs
recorded all our stories.

I am reminded of that Sunday
years ago when we brought the children
to watch two water cooling towers
blown up, recall the appalling void
in the sunlight, like a death.

On this first day of May an icy
rain is blowing through this town,
quieter, cleaner, poorer from today.
The cherries are in flower in Penylan.
Already over East Moors the sky whitens, blind.

Scything

It is blue May. There is work
to be done. The spring's eye blind
with algae, the stopped water
silent. The garden fills
with nettle and briar.
Dylan drags branches away.
I wade forward with my scythe.

There is stickiness on the blade.
Yolk on my hands. Albumen and blood.
Fragments of shell are baby-bones,
the scythe a scalpel, bloodied and guilty
with crushed feathers, mosses, the cut cords
of the grass. We shout at each other
each hurting with a separate pain.

From the crown of the hawthorn tree
to the ground the willow warbler
drops. All day in silence she repeats
her question. I too return
to the place holding the pieces,
at first still hot from the knife,
recall how warm birth fluids are.

Jac Codi Baw

They have torn down in the space of time
it takes to fill a shopping bag,
the building that stood beside my car.
It was grown over with ragwort,
toadflax and buddleia, windows
blind with boarding. Other cars
had time to drive away. Mine
is splattered with the stones' blood, smoky
with ghosts. We are used to the slow
change that weather brings, the gradual
death of a generation, old bricks
crumbling. Inside the car dust lies,
grit in my eyes, in my hair.

He doesn't care. It's a joke to him
clearing space for the pile-drivers,
cheerful in his yellow machine,
cat-calling, laughing at my grief.
But for him too the hand-writing
of a city will be erased.
I can't laugh. Too much comes down
in the deaths of warehouses. Brickdust,
shards of Caernarfon slate. Blood on our hands.

Ram

He died privately.
His disintegration is quiet.
Grass grows among the stems of his ribs,
Ligaments unpicked by the slow rain.
The birds dismantled him for spring nests.
He has spilled himself on the marsh,
His evaporations and his seepings,
His fluids filled a reservoir.
Not long since he could have come
Over the Saddle like a young moon,
His cast shadow whitening Breconshire.

The blue of his eyes is harebell.
Mortality gapes in the craters of his face.
Buzzards cry in the cave of his skull
And a cornucopia of lambs is bleating
Down the Fan of his horns.
In him more of October than rose hips
And bitter sloes. The wind cries drily
Down his nostril bones. The amber
Of his horizontal eye
Is light on reservoir, raven
In winter sky. The sun that creams
The buzzard's belly as she treads air
Whitens his forehead. Flesh
Blackens in the scrolls of his nostrils,
Something of him lingering in bone
Corridors catches my throat.

Seeking a vessel for blackberries and sloes
This helmet would do, were it not filled
Already with its own blacks,
Night in the socket of his eye.

Buzzard

No sutures in the steep brow
of this cranium, as in mine
or yours. Delicate ellipse
as smooth as her own egg

or the cleft flesh of a fruit.
From the plundered bones on the hill,
like a fire in its morning ashes,
you guess it's a buzzard's skull.

You carry it gently home,
hoping no Last Day of the birds
will demand assembly
of her numerous white parts.

In the spaces we can't see
on the other side of walls
as fine as paper, brain and eye
dry out under the gossamers.

Between the sky and the mouse
that moves at the barley field's
spinning perimeter, only
a mile of air and the ganging

crows, their cries stones at her head.
In death, the last stoop, all's risked.
She scorns the scavengers
who feed on death, and never

feel the lightning flash of heart
dropping on heart, warm fur, blood.

Friesian Bull

He blunders through the last dream
of the night. I hear him, waking.
A brick and concrete stall, narrow
as a heifer's haunches. Steel bars
between her trap and his small yard.
A froth of slobbered hay droops
from the stippled muzzle. In the slow
rolling mass of his skull his eyes
surface like fish bellies.

He is chained while they swill his floor.
His stall narrows to rage. He knows
the sweet smell of a heifer's fear.
Remembered summer haysmells reach him,
a trace of the herd's freedom, clover-
loaded winds. The thundering seed
blows up the Dee breathing of plains,
of cattle wading in shallows.
His crazy eyes churn with their vision.

Sunday

Getting up early on a Sunday morning
leaving them sleep for the sake of peace,
the lunch pungent, windows open
for a blackbird singing in Cyncoed.
Starlings glistening in the gutter come
for seed. I let the cats in from the night,
their fur already glossed and warm with March.
I bring the milk, newspaper, settle here
in the bay of the window to watch people
walking to church for Mothering Sunday.
A choirboy holds his robes over his shoulder.
The cats jump up on windowsills to wash
and tremble at the starlings. Like peaty water
sun slowly fills the long brown room.
Opening the paper I admit to this
the war-shriek and starved stare
of a warning I can't name.

Taid's Funeral

From a drawer, a scrap of creased cloth,
an infant's dress of yellowed Viyella
printed with daisies. And a day opens
suddenly as light. The sun is hot.
Grass grows cleanly to a chapel wall.
The stones are rough as a sheepdog's tongue
on the skin of a two-year child.
They allow a fistful of white
gravel, chain her wrists with daisies.

Under the yew tree they lay Taid
in his box like a corm in the ground.

The lawn-mowers are out. Fears repeat
in a conversation of mirrors,
doll within doll; and that old man too small
at last to see, perfect, distinct as a seed.
My hands are cut by silver gravel.
There are dark incisions in the stalks
of the daisies made by a woman's nail.
A new dress stains green with their sap.

Letter From a Far Country

They have gone. The silence resettles
slowly as dust on the sunlit
surfaces of the furniture.
At first the skull itself makes
sounds in any fresh silence,
a big sea running in a shell.
I can hear my blood rise and fall.

Dear husbands, fathers, forefathers,
this is my apologia, my
letter home from the future,
my bottle in the sea which might
take a generation to arrive.

The morning's all activity.
I draw the detritus of a family's
loud life before me, a snow plough,
a road-sweeper with my cart of leaves.
The washing-machine drones
in the distance. From time to time
as it falls silent I fill baskets
with damp clothes and carry them
into the garden, hang them out,
stand back, take pleasure counting
and listing what I have done.
The furniture is brisk with polish.
On the shelves in all of the rooms
I arrange the books
in alphabetical order
according to subject: Mozart,
Advanced Calculus, William
and Paddington Bear.
Into the drawers I place your clean
clothes, pyjamas with buttons
sewn back on, shirts stacked neatly
under their labels on the shelves.

The chests and cupboards are full,
the house sweet as a honeycomb.
I move in and out of the hive
all day, harvesting, ordering.
You will find all in its proper place,
when I have gone.

As I write I am far away.
First see a landscape. Hill country,
essentially feminine,
the sea not far off. Bryn Isaf
down there in the crook of the hill
under Calfaria's single eye.
My grandmother might have lived there.
Any farm. Any chapel.
Father and minister, on guard,
close the white gates to hold her.

A stony track turns between
ancient hedges, narrowing,
like a lane in a child's book.
Its perspective makes the heart restless
like the boy in the rhyme, his stick
and cotton bundle on his shoulder.

The minstrel boy to the war has gone.
But the girl stays. To mind things.
She must keep. And wait. And pass time.

There's always been time on our hands.
We read this perfectly white page
for the black head of the seal,
for the cormorant, as suddenly gone
as a question from the mind,
snaking underneath the surfaces.
A cross of gull shadow on the sea
as if someone stepped on its grave.
After an immeasurable space

the cormorant breaks the surface
as a small, black, returning doubt.

From here the valley is narrow,
the lane lodged like a halfway ledge.
From the opposite wood the birds
ring like a tambourine. It's not
the birdsong of a garden, thrush
and blackbird, robin and finch,
distinguishable, taking turn.
The song's lost in saps and seepings,
amplified by hollow trees,
cupped leaves and wind in the branches.
All their old conversations
collected carefully, faded
and difficult to read, yet held
forever as voices in a well.

Reflections and fallen stones; shouts
into the scared dark of lead-mines;
the ruined warehouse where the owls stare;
sea-caves; cellars; the back stairs
behind the chenille curtain;
the landing when the lights are out;
nightmares in hot feather beds;
the barn where I'm sent to fetch Taid;
that place where the Mellte flows
boldly into limestone caves
and leaps from its hole a mile on,
the nightmare still wild in its voice.

When I was a child a young boy
was drawn into a pipe and drowned
at the swimming pool. I never
forgot him, and pity rivers
inside mountains, and the children
of Hamlyn sucked in by music.
You can hear children crying
from the empty woods.

It's all given back in concert
with the birds and leaves and water
and the song and dance of the Piper.

Listen! to the starlings glistening
on a March morning! Just one day
after snow, an hour after frost,
the thickening grass begins to shine
already in the opening light.
There's wind to rustle the blood,
the sudden flame of crocus.

My grandmother might be standing
in the great silence before the Wars,
hanging the washing between trees
over the white and the red hens.
Sheets. Threadworked pillowcases.
Mamgu's best pais. Her Sunday frock.

The sea stirs restlessly between
the sweetness of clean sheets,
the lifted arms,
the rustling petticoats.

My mother's laundry list, ready
on Mondays when the van called.
The rest soaked in glutinous starch
and whitened with a bluebag
kept in a broken cup.

(In the airing cupboard you'll see
a map, numbering and placing
every towel, every sheet.
I have charted all your needs.)

It has always been a matter
of lists. We have been counting,
folding, measuring, making,
tenderly laundering cloth
ever since we have been women.

The waves are folded meticulously,
perfectly white. Then they are tumbled
and must come to be folded again.

Four herring gulls and their shadows
are shouting at the clear glass
of a shaken wave. The sea's a sheet
bellying in the wind, snapping.
Air and white linen. Our airing cupboards
are full of our satisfactions.

The gulls grieve at our contentment.
It is a masculine question.
"Where" they call "are your great works?"
They slip their fetters and fly up
to laugh at land-locked women.
Their cries are cruel as greedy babies.

Our milky tendernesses dry
to crisp lists; immaculate
linen; jars labelled and glossy
with our perfect preserves.
Spiced oranges; green tomato
chutney; Seville orange marmalade
annually staining gold
the snows of January.

(The saucers of marmalade
are set when the amber wrinkles
like the sea if you blow it.)

Jams and jellies of blackberry,
crabapple, strawberry, plum,
greengage and loganberry.
You can see the fruit pressing
their little faces against the glass;
tiny onions imprisoned
in their preservative juices.

Familiar days are stored whole
in bottles. There's a wet morning
orchard in the dandelion wine;
a white spring distilled
in elderflower's clarity;
and a loving, late, sunburning
day of October in syrups
of rose hip and the beautiful
black sloes that stained the gin to rose.

It is easy to make of love
these ceremonials. As priests
we fold cloth, break bread, share wine,
hope there's enough to go round.

(You'll find my inventories pinned
inside all of the cupboard doors).

Soon they'll be planting the barley.
I imagine I see it, stirring
like blown sand, feel the stubble
cutting my legs above blancoed
daps in a summer too hot
for Wellingtons. The cans of tea
swing squeakily on wire loops,
outheld, not to scald myself,
over the ten slow leagues
of the field of golden knives.
To be out with the men, at work,
I had longed to carry their tea,

for the feminine privilege,
for the male right to the field.
Even that small task made me bleed.
Halfway between the flowered lap
of my grandmother and the black
heraldic silhouette of men
and machines on the golden field,
I stood crying, my ankle bones
raw and bleeding like the poppies
trussed in the corn stooks in their torn
red silks and soft mascara blacks.

(The recipe for my best bread,
half granary meal, half strong brown flour,
water, sugar, yeast and salt,
is copied out in the small black book).

In the black book of this parish
a hundred years ago
you will find the unsupported
woman had "pauper" against her name.
She shared it with old men.

The parish was rich with movement.
The woollen mills were spinning.
Water-wheels milled the sunlight
and the loom's knock was a heart
behind all activity.
The shuttles were quick as birds
in the warp of the oakwoods.
In the fields the knives were out
in a glint of husbandry.
In back bedrooms, barns and hedges,
in hollows of the hills,
the numerous young were born.

The people were at work:
dressmaker; wool carder; quilter;
midwife; farmer; apprentice;
house servant; scholar; labourer;
shepherd; stocking knitter; tailor;
carpenter; mariner; ploughman;
wool spinner; cobbler; cottager;
Independent Minister.

And the paupers: Enoch Elias
and Ann, his wife; David Jones,
Sarah and Esther their daughter;
Mary Evans and Ann Tanrallt;
Annie Cwm March and child;
Eleanor Thomas, widow, Crug Glas;
Sara Jones, 84, and daughter;
Nicholas Rees, aged 80, and his wife;
Mariah Evans the Cwm, widow;
on the parish for want of work.
Housebound by infirmity, age,
widowhood, or motherhood.

Before the Welfare State who cared
for sparrows in a hard spring?

The stream's cleaner now; it idles
past derelict mill-wheels; the drains
do its work. Since the tanker sank
the unfolding rose of the sea
blooms on the beaches, wave on wave
black, track-marked, each tide
a procession of the dead.
Slack water's treacherous; each veined
wave is a stain in seal-milk;
the sea gapes, hopelessly
licking itself.

(Examine your hands
scrupulously
for signs of dirt in your own blood.
And wash them before meals).

In that innocent smallholding
where the swallows live and field mice
winter and the sheep barge in
under the browbone, the windows
are blind, are doors for owls,
bolt-holes for dreams. The thoughts have flown.
The last death was a suicide.
The lowing cows discovered her,
the passing-bell of their need
warned a winter morning that day
when no one came to milk them.
Later, they told me, a baby
was born in the room where she died,
as if by this means sanctified,
a death outcried by a birth.
Middle-aged, poor, isolated,
she could not recover
from mourning an old parent's death.
Influenza brought an hour
too black, too narrow to escape.

More mysterious to them
was the woman who had everything.
A village house with railings;
rooms of good furniture;
fine linen in the drawers;
a garden full of herbs and flowers;
a husband in work; grown sons.
She had a cloud on her mind,
they said, and her death shadowed them.
It couldn't be explained.

I watch for her face looking out,
small and white, from every window,
like a face in a jar. Gossip,
whispers, lowing sounds. Laughter.

The people have always talked.
The landscape collects conversations
as carefully as a bucket,
gives them back in concert
with a wood of birdsong.

(If you hear your name in that talk
don't listen. Eavesdroppers never
heard anything good of themselves).

When least expected you catch
the eye of the enemy
looking coldly from the old world...
Here's a woman who ought to be
up to her wrists in marriage;
not content with the second hand
she is shaking the bracelets
from her arms. The sea circles
her ankles. Watch its knots loosen
from the delicate bones
of her feet, from the rope of foam
about a rock. The seal swims
in a collar of water
drawing the horizon in its wake.
And doubt breaks the perfect
white surface of the day.

About the tree in the middle
of the cornfield the loop of gold
is loose as water; as the love
we should bear one another.

When I rock the sea rocks. The moon
doesn't seem to be listening
invisible in a pale sky,
keeping a light hand on the rein.

Where is woman in this trinity?
The mare who draws the load?
The hand on the leather?
The cargo of wheat?

Watching sea-roads I feel
the tightening white currents,
am waterlogged, my time set
to the sea's town clock.
My cramps and drownings, energies,
desires draw the loaded net
of the tide over the stones.

A lap full of pebbles and then
light as a Coca Cola can.
I am freight. I am ship.
I cast ballast overboard.
The moon decides my Equinox.
At high tide I am leaving.

The women are leaving.
They are paying their taxes
and dues. Filling in their passports.
They are paying to Caesar
what is Caesar's, to God what is God's,
To Woman what is Man's.

I hear the dead grandmothers,
Mamgu from Ceredigion,
Nain from the North, all calling
their daughters down from the fields,
calling me in from the road.
They haul at the taut silk cords;

set us fetching eggs, feeding hens,
mixing rage with the family bread,
lock us to the elbows in soap suds.
Their sculleries and kitchens fill
with steam, sweetnesses, goosefeathers.

On the graves of my grandfathers
the stones, in their lichens and mosses,
record each one's importance.
Diaconydd. Trysorydd.
Pillars of their society.
Three times at chapel on Sundays.
They are in league with the moon
but as silently stony
as the simple names of their women.

We are hawks trained to return
to the lure from the circle's
far circumference. Children sing
that note that only we can hear.
The baby breaks the waters,
disorders the blood's tune, sets
each filament of the senses
wild. Its cry tugs at flesh, floods
its mother's milky fields.
Nightly in white moonlight I wake
from sleep one whole slow minute
before the hungry child
wondering what woke me.

School's out. The clocks strike four.
Today this letter goes unsigned,
unfinished, unposted.
When it is finished
I will post it from a far country.

If we launch the boat and sail away
Who will rock the cradle? Who will stay?
If women wander over the sea
Who'll be home when you come in for tea?

If we go hunting along with the men
Who will light the fires and bake bread then?
Who'll catch the nightmares and ride them away
If we put to sea and we sail away?

Will the men grow tender and the children strong?
Who will teach the Mam iaith and sing them songs?
If we adventure more than a day
Who will do the loving while we're away?

Kingfishers at Condat

Our hair still damp from swimming,
heads full of deep brown water
reflecting with reeds, we drink
an apéritif in Condat.

At the heart of the village silence
of gold-dust and evening heat
the café is full of youths
in leather for motor-cycling.

Their bikes wait in the courtyard,
blue as mallard, glittering flies
taking nourishment from dust,
at rest from their buzzing and fuss.

Excluded, uneasy at their stares
and the outbreak of laughter, we carry
our drinks outside, read their newspaper
in revenge, like a bill of right.

Out here on the parapet
the stone has absorbed September.
We sit alone, sweetnesses
of the wine on our mouths and fingers.

Their laughter is distant. The river
moves its surfaces, its reedy
stirrings and sudden glitter
rushing under the bridge.

Downstream the Coly, where we swam,
Meets the Vézère in a wide
confluence, deceivingly
cool under the evening's gold.

The yard is loud with boys. With us
for audience, one by one they go
roaring and glittering into the trees.
The river moves in peace, and there!

under the bank where it's dark, blue
as fire the kingfishers are hunting,
blue as storm, iridescent, alive
to the quoit on the surface

where the fish rises. Dragonfly
blue crackling down the dark vein
of the riverbank, as quick
and as private as joy.

Seamstress at St Léon

As we eat crushed strawberry ice
under a bee-heavy vine
we watch for the seamstress to come.
Through the open doorway we hear
her chatter, see her Singers
glint with gold roses in the dark room.

Embroidery cloths abandoned
at the roadside table; a weir
of lace falls from her chair; silks
spill blossoming from a basket.
Under its turning ribbon of gauze
her tea cools in a white cup.

She sings in the dark interior.
From the sills of the gardenless house
fuchsia and geranium blaze.
Her windows are framed with French knots,
the cracks seeded with lazy daisy.
Her rubber plant reaches the eaves.

Nothing troubles the afternoon dust
or breaks the tenor of bees
but her counterpoint. Out of sight
in their web of scaffolding
under the bridge, workmen whistle
and a hammer rings over water.

A fan of shadow slowly includes us.
Her tea is cold. Imperceptibly
the thicket of roses grows closer.
We make out the sinuous gilding
of sewing machines, vine leaves, stems
and iron tendrils of their treadles.

Lace glimmerings at dusk. A foam
of linen, flowers, silences.
Sunlight has flowed from her sills
of yellow stone. Bats are shuttling
their delicate black silks to mesh
that dark doorway on her absence.

Rouffignac

In the forest overhead
summer fruit is falling
like the beat of a drum.

Hold your breath and you hear
millennia of water
sculpting limestone.

The river runs in the heat
of the sun. We are walking
in its grave, imagine

a throat choking with water,
a power drill at work. Vast
cupolas prove its turbulence.

I am not deceived
by the nursery frieze
of mammoth. The circus act

brings on the bison,
black and ochre
ponies on terra cotta.

The Vézère is a ghost,
its footprints everywhere.
Even the kitchen taps

run cloudy into the palms
of our hands, fill our mouths
with chalk.

Font de Gaume

Fourteen thousand years make little difference.
Some of us, finding smooth places in the rough
must carve there, using old water marks.
A stalactite for a horse's thigh, its eye
a fault, or where the river fingered a whorl
a vortex turned the doorways of the skull.
Sinews of calcite, muscles run and slack,
the belly droops, a boulder marbles bone.

The imagination's caverns cry for symbols,
shout to the hot sun in the present tense.
We walk again in the afternoon,
watch out for vipers lazy on their stones.
Two tractors are towing home the harvest.
Tobacco saps evaporate in rows.
The glittering Vézère is at its work,
its inexhaustible calligraphy.

Brother, grinding your colours by tallow light,
I hear your heart beat under my collarbone.

Heron at Port Talbot

Snow falls on the cooling towers
delicately settling on cranes.
Machinery's old bones whiten; death
settles with its rusts, its erosions.

Warning of winds off the sea
the motorway dips to the dock's edge.
My hands tighten on the wheel against
the white steel of the wind.

Then we almost touch, both braking flight,
bank on the air and feel that shocking
intimacy of near-collision,
animal tracks that cross in snow.

I see his living eye, his change of mind,
feel pressure as we bank, the force
of his beauty. We might have died
in some terrible conjunction.

The steel town's sulphurs billow
like dirty washing. The sky stains
with steely inks and fires, chemical
rustings, salt-grains, sand under snow.

And the bird comes, a surveyor
calculating space between old workings
and the mountain hinterland, archangel
come to re-open the heron-roads,

meets me at an inter-section
where wind comes flashing off water
interrupting the warp of the snow
and the broken rhythms of blood.

Suicide on Pentwyn Bridge

I didn't know him,
the man who jumped from the bridge.
But I saw the parabola
of long-drawn-out falling in the brown

eyes of his wife week after week
at the supermarket cash-out.
We would quietly ask "How is he?"
hear of the hospital's white

care, the corridors between her
and the broken man in the bed,
and the doctors who had no words,
no common supermarket women's talk.

Only after the funeral
I knew how he'd risen, wild
from his chair and told her
he was going out to die.

Very slowly from the first leap
he fell through winter, through the cold
of Christmas, wifely silences,
the blue scare of ambulance,

from his grave on the motorway
to the hospital, two bridges down.
A season later in a slow cortège
he has reached the ground.

Plums

When their time comes they fall
without wind, without rain.
They seep through the trees' muslin
in a slow fermentation.

Daily the low sun warms them
in a late love that is sweeter
than summer. In bed at night
we hear heartbeat of fruitfall.

The secretive slugs crawl home
to the burst honeys, are found
in the morning mouth on mouth,
inseparable.

We spread patchwork counterpanes
for a clean catch. Baskets fill,
never before such harvest,
such a hunters' moon burning

the hawthorns, drunk on syrups
that are richer by night
when spiders pitch
tents in the wet grass.

This morning the red sun
is opening like a rose
on our white wall, prints there
the fishbone shadow of a fern.

The early blackbirds fly
guilty from a dawn haul
of fallen fruit. We too
breakfast on sweetnesses.

Soon plum trees will be bone,
grown delicate with frost's
formalities. Their black
angles will tear the snow.

Death of a Cat

His nightmare rocked the house
but no one woke, accustomed
to the heart's disturbances.

We dug a grave last night
under the apple tree where fruit
fattens in green clusters.

Black and white fur perfect
except where soil fell
or where small blood seeped

between the needles of her teeth
in the cracked china of her bones.
Perfect but for darkness

clotting the skull and silence
like the note of an organ
hanging in the locked air.

Dylan dreamed it again,
woken by caterwauling.
Two mourners held a wake

at dawn on the compost heap
(her special place) yowling
to wake the sleeping and to stop

the heart, considering
animal mysteries,
the otherness of pain.

He watched, from the window,
the dawn moon dissolving
its wafer on the tongue.

Cardiff Elms

Until this summer
through the open roof of the car
their lace was light as rain
against the burning sun.
On a rose-coloured road
they laid their inks,
knew exactly, in the seed,
where in the sky they would reach
precise parameters.

Traffic-jammed under a square
of perfect blue I thirst
for their lake's fingering
shadow, trunk by trunk arching
a cloister between the parks
and pillars of a civic architecture,
older and taller than all of it.

Heat is a salt encrustation.
Walls square up to the sky
without the company of leaves
or the town life of birds.
At the roadside this enormous
firewood, elmwood, the start
of some terrible undoing.

Sheila na Gig at Kilpeck

Pain's a cup of honey in the pelvis.
She burns in the long, hot afternoon, stone
among the monstrous nursery faces
circling Kilpeck church. Those things we notice
as we labour distantly revolve
outside her perpetual calendar.
Men in the fields. Loads following the lanes,
strands of yellow hair caught in the hedges.

The afternoon turns round us.
The beat of the heart a great tongue in its bell,
a swell between bone cliffs; restlessness
that sets me walking; that second sight
of shadows crossing cornfields. We share
premonitions, are governed by moons
and novenas, sisters cooling our wrists
in the stump of a Celtic water stoop.

Not lust but long labouring
absorbs her, mother of the ripening
barley that swells and frets at its walls.
Somewhere far away the Severn presses,
alert at flood-tide. And everywhere rhythms
are turning their little gold cogs, caught
in her waterfalling energy.

Siege

I waste the sun's last hour, sitting here
at the kitchen window. Tea and a pile
of photographs to sort. Radio news
like smoke of conflagrations far away.
There isn't room for another petal
or leaf out there, this year of blossom.
Light dazzles the hedge roots underneath
the heavy shadows, burns the long grass.

I, in my father's arms in this garden
with dandelion hair. He, near forty,
unaccustomed to the restlessness
of a baby's energy. Small hands
tear apart the photograph's composure.
She pushes his chest to be let down
where daisies embroider his new shoes.

Perfumes and thorns are tearing
from the red may tree. Wild white Morello
and a weeping cherry heavy in flower.
The lilac slowly shows. Small oaks spread
their gestures. Poplars glisten. Pleated green
splits black husks of ash. Magnolia
drops its wax. Forsythia
fallen like a yellow dress.
Underfoot daisies from a deep
original root burst the darkness.

My mother, posing in a summer dress
in the corn at harvest time. Her brothers,
shadowy middle distance figures,
stoop with pitchforks to lift the sheaves.
Out of sight Captain, or Belle, head fallen
to rest in the lee of the load, patient
for the signal. Out of heart too the scare
of the field far down from the sunstruck top

of the load, and the lurch at the gate
as we ditch and sway left down the lane.

The fallen sun lies low in the bluebells.
It is nearly summer. Midges hang
in the air. A wren is singing, sweet
in a lilac tree. Thrushes hunt the lawn,
eavesdrop for stirrings in the daisy roots.
The wren repeats her message distantly.
In a race of speedwell over grass
the thrushes are silently listening.
A yellow butterfly begins
its unsteady journey over the lawn.

The radio voices break and suddenly
the garden burns, is full of barking dogs.
A woman screams and gunsmoke blossoms
in the apple trees. Sheaves of fire
are scorching the grass and in my kitchen
is a roar of floors falling, machine guns.

The wren moves closer and repeats that song
of lust and burgeoning. Never clearer
the figures standing on the lawn, sharpnesses
of a yellow butterfly, almost there.

Llŷr

Ten years old, at my first Stratford play:
The river and the king with their Welsh names
Bore in the darkness of a summer night
Through interval and act and interval.
Swans moved double through glossy water
Gleaming with imponderable meanings.
Was it Gielgud on that occasion?
Or ample Laughton, crazily white-gowned,
Pillowed in wheatsheaves on a wooden cart,
Who taught the significance of little words?
All. Nothing. Fond. Ingratitude. Words
To keep me scared, awake at night. That old
Man's vanity and a daughter's "Nothing",
Ran like a nursery rhythm in my head.

Thirty years later on the cliffs of Llŷn
I watch how Edgar's crows and choughs still measure
How high cliffs are, how thrown stones fall
Into history, how deeply the bruise
Spreads in the sea where the wave has broken.
The turf is stitched with tormentil and thrift,
Blue squill and bird bones, tiny shells, heartsease.
Yellowhammers sing like sparks in the gorse.
The landscape's marked with figures of old men:
The bearded sea; thin-boned, wind-bent trees;
Shepherd and labourer and night-fisherman.
Here and there among the crumbling farms
Are lit kitchen windows on distant hills,
And guilty daughters longing to be gone.

Night falls on Llŷn, on forefathers,
Old Celtic kings and the more recent dead,
Those we are still guilty about, flowers
Fade in jam jars on their graves; renewed
Refusals are heavy on our minds.
My head is full of sound, remembered speech,

Syllables, ideas just out of reach;
The close, looped sound of curlew and the far
Subsidiary roar, cadences shaped
By the long coast of the peninsula,
The continuous pentameter of the sea.
When I was ten a fool and a king sang
Rhymes about sorrow, and there I heard
That nothing is until it has a word.

Blodeuwedd

Hours too soon a barn owl
broke from woodshadow.
Her white face rose
out of darkness
in a buttercup field.

Colourless and soundless, feathers
cream as meadowsweet
and oakflowers, condemned
to the night, to lie alone
with her sin.

Deprived too of afternoons
in the comfortable sisterhood
of women moving in kitchens
among cups, cloths and running
water while they talk,

as we three talk tonight
in Hendre, the journey over.
We pare and measure and stir,
heap washed apples in a bowl, recall
the day's work, our own fidelities.

Her night lament
beyond conversation,
the owl follows
her shadow like a cross
over the fields,

Blodeuwedd's ballad
where the long reach
of the peninsula
is black in a sea
aghast with gazing.

Bluetit and Wren

Two of all those
That have lived in our wall
left us their meanings.

The bluetit found
after bitter winter,
yellow feathers

just reachable, blue down
at fingertip, beak turned
to breast as though

the sky that called her
to build among stones froze her
to ammonite.

And the brown wren
who whirred from her cave as I
repeatedly

turned the corner
with a shovel of fresh mortar
for your pointing.

We met there, placed
our fingers in the wren's nest
holding our breath

at mossy heat,
the delicate tiny eggs
each with its pulse.

Such secret interiors.

Blodeuyn

The dark wound in the corn
is a right of way through barley.
The first fine evening after summer floods
we wade waist deep in it.
Pattern of bright barley in my hand
exactly shadowed in deep tyre tracks
that barley-print the mud.

We follow Lloyd in the dusk
through corn into beech trees, a sunken
lane, only the dry risen stones,
white underfoot, to show the way.
Blodeuyn at the dark lane's end,
flowers fallen, as purples fall
from husks of August foxgloves.

A longhouse crouching on the long
white bones of beech trees, empty
sixty years, an animal quiet
in it, of old women stooping
at the door they shared with cattle.
My clogs on cobbles muffle theirs.
Birds scare from the eye sockets.

We turn for home up the muddy fosse,
cross the pale field diagonally.
First stars. The harebell-thin thread
of a distant tree. In the dusk
the moon's delicate skull watches
while we stumble home through smells
of the barley's bowed wet heads,
Blodeuyn's silence in us.

Shadows in Llanbadarn

All shadows on the wall are blue.
Ladder-shadow. The rope askew
on the tenth rung. The Manx kitten
leaping the gap to the orchard wall.
Yours, searching the February soil
for points of green. Papery brown
flowers of dead hydrangea stir.

From the wall to the tenth rung
the kitten drops and settles, fur
black and tiger-barred with black,
tense at the rope a breath scares.
In her face the sudden sticky green
of buds in darkness burns with sun.
Your shadow turns. I hear it on the stair.

The ladder's last. The falling sun
gradually drowns it, rung by rung.

The Water-Diviner

His fingers tell water like prayer.
He hears its voice in the silence
through fifty feet of rock
on an afternoon dumb with drought.

Under an old tin bath, a stone,
an upturned can, his copper pipe
glints with discovery. We dip our hose
deep into the dark, sucking its dryness,

till suddenly the water answers,
not the little sound we know,
but a thorough bass too deep
for the naked ear, shouts through the hose

a word we could not say, or spell, or remember,
something like "dŵr. . .dŵr".

Syphoning the Spring

We have struggled all day to syphon water.

This morning, the air blue and the damp,
the wet, the glitter of water rose
through our fingers from a hose
dipped into drilled rock.
But the hose isn't long enough nor the hill
steep enough for water to come.
For an hour it falters in the bed of the stream
among wild forgetmenots, tracing water-veins
with their hint of mist, of water-breath.
Then we bind the pump to the hose again
and pump and pump till the bubble of rubber fills
with certain water, then drive the handle down.

Through flared fingers the water comes
like birth-water, catching green light
of fern and cresses and blue forgetmenots.

While we are sleeping
water moves in moonlight,
a slow pulse in the shallows.
Some time in the night it will stop,
in the dead hour when people die,
till we borrow more hose, find a steeper hill
so that it dares to fall clear, for it wants
to fall, to give itself, knowing the risk.

Missa Pontcanna

Forty years confined
in the sisterhood of silence. Noise to her
was chink of rosary, footfall
on gravel in a walled garden,
trapped song of blackbird
the hour before Angelus.

In a world unimagined before today
she shared the night with a crowd gathering
in darkness like a great migration,
the dawn moon dissolving,
the rose-window of the rising sun.

She has known in one dazzling day
circus and seaside, fair-day and birthday,
oratorio, picnic, holy day, holiday,
crowd, Kyrie, caritas, caru,
and a Pope behind glass, his smile distant
after television's intimacy.

First sight of the world —
a hundred thousand picnic by a river,
the old faint in the heat, the young
sunbathe profanely, diving for joy in the Taff.
First sound after silence a crowd's roar
under yellow flags like barley in wind.

Catching her patience the Taff loiters
in shadow, falls in a wimple of pleats
over Blackweir counting its prayer on stones.
Dizzy, sunburnt, as at the close of any
secular day, they queue for the bridge.
Thunder growls and the rain begins.

Something is over. In the cell of herself
the day stores its honey and an image
of the world for whose salvation
she tells and tells her beads.

My Box

My box is made of golden oak,
my lover's gift to me.
He fitted hinges and a lock
of brass and a bright key.
He made it out of winter nights,
sanded and oiled and planed,
engraved inside the heavy lid
in brass, a golden tree.

In my box are twelve black books
where I have written down
how we have sanded, oiled and planed,
planted a garden, built a wall,
seen jays and goldcrests, rare red kites,
found the wild heartsease, drilled a well,
harvested apples and words and days
and planted a golden tree.

On an open shelf I keep my box.
Its key is in the lock.
I leave it there for you to read,
or them, when we are dead,
how everything is slowly made,
how slowly things made me,
a tree, a lover, words, a box,
books and a golden tree.

Mass of the Birds

Frances, this morning,
buttercup dust on our sandals,
we drift back from early walks,
bring roses in long briars,
foxglove, bedstraw, meadowsweet,
cow parsley, ragged robin.

The mist is off the fields. Swifts
spin their shrill litanies.
Under the barn's beaten silver
incense of cut grass, creosote,
the sun's mat at the door.
We bring our privacies.

Rough table. Circle of chairs.
A heel of granary loaf.
Wine over from last night's supper.
A leather book. Luke. Romans.
Corinthians. Silences.
A congregation of eight.

The lapsed, the doubting, those
here for the first time, others
regular at named churches
share the meaning of breaking bread,
of sipping from one glass,
of naming you.

Mass of the birds. A blackbird calls,
a wren responds, calling, answering
what we can only feel.
We offer this as the sun
raises its wafer too brilliant
to look at or understand.

Do you remember the elder
that was sick to death last year,
all skin and bone in the arms
of a rambling rose? This year
it flourishes, grows green,
supports the rose.

A Dream of Horses

I dreamed a gallop across sand
in and out the scallop of the tide
on a colourless horse as cold as a seal.

My hair and the mane of the horse
are the long white manes of the sea.
Every breath is a gulp of salt.

Now we are ocean. His hoof-prints
are pools, his quivering skin
the silk in the trough of the wave.

His muscular ellipses are
the sinuous long water of the sea
and I swim with the waves in my arms.

October

Wind in the poplars and a broken branch,
a dead arm in the bright trees. Five poplars
tremble gradually to gold. The stone face
of the lion darkens in a sharp shower,
his dreadlocks of lobelia grown long,
tangled, more brown now than blue-eyed.

My friend dead and the graveyard at Orcop —
her short ride to the hawthorn hedge, lighter
than hare-bones on men's shoulders, our faces
stony, rain, weeping in the air. The grave
deep as a well takes the earth's thud, the slow
fall of flowers.

                    Over the page the pen
runs faster than wind's white steps over grass.
For a while health feels like pain. Then panic
running the fields, the grass, the racing leaves
ahead of light, holding that robin's eye
in the laurel, hydrangeas' faded green.
I must write like the wind, year after year
passing my death-day, winning ground.

Fires on Llŷn

At sunset we climb Uwchmynydd
to a land's end
where R.S. Thomas walks, finding
the footprint of God
warm in the shoe of the hare.

Words shape-shift to wind, a flight
of oystercatchers,
whinchat on a bush, two cormorants
fast-dipping wings
in a brilliant sea.

Over the holy sound Enlli
is dark in a ruff
of foam. Any pebble or shell
might be the knuckle-bone
or vertebra of a saint.

Three English boys throw stones.
Choughs sound alarm.
Sea-birds rise and twenty thousand saints
finger the shingle
to the sea's intonation.

Facing west, we've talked for hours
of our history,
thinking of Ireland and the hurt
cities,
gunshot on lonely farms,

praised unsectarian saints,
Enlli open
to the broken rosary
of their coracles,
praying in Latin and Welsh.

Done with cliff-talking we turn
inland, thinking
of home silently filling
with shadows, the hearth
quiet for the struck match,

our bed spread with clean sheets.
Our eyes are tired
with sun-gazing. Suddenly
we shout — the farms burn.
Through binoculars we see

distant windows curtained with flame.
The fires are real
that minute while we gasp, begin
to run, then realise
windows catch, not fire but

the setting sun. We are struck still
without a word
in any language. See the hares run,
windows darken,
hear the sea's mumbled novenas.

Climbing Cader Idris

(for a mountaineer)

You know the mountain with your body,
I with my mind, I suppose.
Each, in our way, describes
the steepening angle of rock.

What difference now as we,
falling into step and conversation,
put to the test our long
thigh muscles and our breath,

turning together to the open view,
a distant plough, a lozenge of field.
We face the slope again, our boots
rough-riding the scree up, up. . . .

. . . .past the last ruined hafod, the last flower,
stream falling among boulders,
the mountain ewe and her lamb and at last
Llyn Cau like a secret cupped in hands.

You climb on to the summit
"to test my body further".
I prefer to stare at shirred water
and the vast face of stone.

I search for words.
While I'm still catching my breath
you describe that dizzy joy
at the sheer page,

"A move so delicate
along a traverse,
just fingertip
between the hold and the fall".

Castell y Bere

So many deaths under unfurling trees
or on banks where primrose makes us dizzy
after ten miles of mountain track —

a lamb's head clean as a toy, the beads
of its vertebrae picked smooth as hail maries,
hobby horse, head on a stake, Llywelyn
shorn of his coat to mother-smell an orphan
for the grieving ewe.

In the barn that other lamb
a husk in my hands, delicate and swift
as a chalk horse, its four hooves galloping
no-where forever in its attitude
of birth, stillborn on its journey, still
in the caul of its skin, not skeleton
but bas-relief, little sea-horse, womb-horse.

In the wood the jay's discarded robe,
barred-blue wing-feathers, fallen black arrows
of flight, breast-down cream, rose, terra cotta,
a quiver of feathers, a drop of fresh blood
in calm afternoon but no bird at all.

Then the kestrel on its back in torchlight
dead with Tonfannau's ghostly soldiery
in the deserted military camp.
On a concrete floor littered with glass
and owl-pellets, his royal feathers dressed
impeccably black and gold as heraldry.
His turned head is a skull, his breast
a seethe of hatching spiders.

Epithalamium

(for Anne Stevenson and Michael Farley)

Skylark crazy in the tall air.
Bluetit busy at the wall
where old earth-mortar falls
from between stones.

Willow-warblers, piccolo and flute.
One is a dash of light
from sycamore to ash,
hawthorn to beech.

The other follows, a glass
of blinding brilliance as one
car windscreen, bees-wing or blade of grass
suddenly couples with the sun.

We are dusty with gardening.
My fingers taste of starch
from cutting seed potatoes.
You call from Cardiff, telling

of your wedding in my city.
We drink to you with sour sherry.
Meg rolls in speedwell and comes up for air
with brideflowers in her ears.

The warblers are still. One brings
the first feather. The other sings
the first calm courtship minute
and begins to build.

Today

Kate in full day in the heat of the sun
looks into the grave, sees in that unearthing
of a Roman settlement, under a stone
only the shadow of a skeleton.

Gwyn on his back in the dark, lying
on the lawn dry from months of drought,
finds in the sky through the telescope
the fuzzy dust of stars he had been searching.

Imprint of bones is a constellation
shining against silence, against darkness,
and stars are the pearly vertebrae
of water-drops against the drought, pelvis,

skull, scapula five million light years old
wink in the glass, and stardust is all we hold
of the Roman lady's negative
in the infinite dark of the grave.

The Hare

(i.m. Frances Horovitz 1938-1983)

That March night I remember how we heard
a baby crying in a neighbouring room
but found him sleeping quietly in his cot.

The others went to bed and we sat late
talking of children and the men we loved.
You thought you'd like another child. "Too late"

you said. And we fell silent, thought a while
of yours with his copper hair and mine,
a grown daughter and sons.

Then, that joke we shared, our phases of the moon.
"Sisterly lunacy" I said. You liked
the phrase. It became ours. Different

as earth and air, yet in one trace that week
we towed the calends like boats reining
the oceans of the world at the full moon.

Suddenly from the fields we heard again
a baby cry, and standing at the door
listened for minutes, ears and eyes soon used

to the night. It was cold. In the east
the river made a breath of shining sound.
The cattle in the field were shadow black.

A cow coughed. Some slept, and some pulled grass.
I could smell blossom from the blackthorn
and see their thorny crowns against the sky.

And then again, a sharp cry from the hill.
"A hare", we said together, not speaking
of fox or trap that held it in a lock

of terrible darkness. Both admitted
next day to lying guilty hours awake
at the crying of the hare. You told me

of sleeping at last in the jaws of a bad dream.
''I saw all the suffering of the world
in a single moment. Then I heard

a voice say 'But this is nothing, nothing
to the mental pain'.'' I couldn't speak of it.
I thought about your dream when you lay ill.

In the last heavy nights before full moon,
when its face seems sorrowful and broken,
I look through binoculars. Its seas flower

like clouds over water, it wears its craters
like silver rings. Even in dying you
menstruated as a woman in health

considering to have a child or no.
When they hand me insults or little hurts
and I'm on fire with my arguments

at your great distance you can calm me still.
Your dream, my sleeplessness, the cattle
asleep under a full moon,

and out there
the dumb and stiffening body of the hare.

Overheard in County Sligo

I married a man from County Roscommon
and I live at the back of beyond
with a field of cows and a yard of hens
and six white geese on the pond.

At my door's a square of yellow corn
caught up by its corners and shaken,
and the road runs down through the open gate
and freedom's there for the taking.

I had thought to work on the Abbey stage
or have my name in a book,
to see my thought on the printed page,
or still the crowd with a look.

But I turn to fold the breakfast cloth
and to polish the lustre and brass,
to order and dust the tumbled rooms
and find my face in the glass.

I ought to feel I'm a happy woman
for I lie in the lap of the land,
and I married a man from County Roscommon
and I live in the back of beyond.

Taid's Grave

Rain on lilac leaves. In the dusk
they show me the grave,
a casket of stars underfoot,
his name there, and his language.

Voice of thrushes in rain.
My cousin Gwynfor eases me
into the green cave.
Wet hands of lilac

touch my wrist and the secret
unfreckled underside of my arm
daring fingers to count
five warm blue eggs.

All Souls' Night

Wind after rain. The lane
is beaten lead. Nothing

is any colour. Hedges
are scribbles of darkness.

Not a cow or sheep in grey fields.
Rain sings in the culverts,

slides the gate-bars, brambles and grasses,
glints in tyre-ruts and hoof-prints.

Only the springer's fur flowers white,
will o' the wisp under a gate

across a field short-sightedly
reading the script of the fox.

A sudden wheel of starlings turns
the hill's corner, their wings a whish

of air, the darkening sound
of a shadow crossing land.

At a touch my bare ash tree rings,
leafed, shaken,

the stopper of ice dissolved
in each bird-throat,

the frozen ash
become a burning bush.

Spaniel

Between the two of us
everything is more.
About the stern commands —
fetch, lie, stay —
or the clear images —
ball, stick, bed —
are the qualifying clauses,
muscular syntax
that helps me think aloud.
My voice speaks what her tongue,
tail, racing feet say too.
Across the fields she runs
nose down to the sinuous
language of smell
telling the secret
inbetween things of speech.

Together we find a hare
killed on the road.
She knows its nightly track,
its way of death, who plundered it
and where, on paws, on wings they fled.
While she is wild and trembles
with the night's history,
I am stilled by its myth.
With my boot I gently
roll the dead hare
to the dignity of the ditch.
Because she thinks I am wise
she is silent, still, wide-eyed.

Marged

I think of her sometimes when I lie in bed,
falling asleep in the room I have made in the roof-space
over the old dark parlŵr where she died
alone in winter, ill and penniless.
Lighting the lamps, November afternoons,
a reading book, whisky gold in my glass.
At my type-writer tapping under stars
at my new roof-window, radio tunes
and dog for company. Or parking the car
where through the mud she called her single cow
up from the field, under the sycamore.
Or looking at the hills she looked at too.
I find her broken crocks, digging her garden.
What else do we share, but being women?

Tawny Owl

Plain song of owl
moonlight between cruciform
shadows of hunting.

She sings again
closer
in the sycamore,

her coming quieter
than the wash
behind the wave,

her absence darker
than privacy
in the leaves' tabernacle.

Compline. Vigil.
Stations of the dark.
A flame floats on oil

in her amber eye.
Shoulderless shadow
nightwatching.

Kyrie. Kyrie.

Tadzekistan

From the little plane
to Samarkand, rickety as a toy,
through gauzy heat a green geometry
glitters with miraculous white roses
of water on their silver conduits.

The image jumps
like old film under the rattling wing.
The desert, not gold as in children's books,
but mountainous and grey with stone-dust,
the cotton-fields laid out like carpets,

prayer rugs in the drought.
Walking, later, in the hot ash
of the ancient desert city, I see
the impossible silver battlements
of distant glaciers, and in the valley

water's quicksilver,
its Catherine wheels, its memory
of fern-designs that lean in wet places,
of feathers dropping from water-birds,
of dizzy vortices that know the way to spin.

It is melted mountain
come so far in the dark pipes and channels.
Yet it learns again the colour of the ice
it was. From here we look from the precipice,
hear a dog bark, a child cry, a cockerel crow,

see a Tadzek woman hang
clean cotton in the sun like any wife.
Let us praise hydro-engineers and five-year plans.
Let us praise the designer of ice-mountains glittering blue
on a far horizon like a wild idea.

Shearing

No trouble finding them. Their cries
rise with the wind along the lane
spiced with hawthorn and golden chain.

A shovel turning snow, the blade
slides under the filthy fleece
to sugar-almond flesh,

turning the wool's silver, spreads it
in the dirt of the barn, whole,
wide as a double quilt.

In the orchard the ewes grieve.
Warm winds herd them, begin
to heal their nakedness.

A sheepdog with silver eyes
listens for cries and silences
under trailing electric flexes.

At tea-break we rest, the smells of wool
like wet Burberries going home from school
delayed in woods by a pool of sticklebacks,

that space between two activities
where something is lost and somebody's
footsteps are following you home.

And innocently, helping Nanna,
I pass tea to the thin, dark man
in the blue boiler-suit and move on,

take out my camera for a picture
of shearing-day, Hywel, Nanna,
and helpers from neighbouring farms.

Next day, still in my camera not smiling,
he died in a noose in his own barn
leaving Hywel his moon-eyed dog.

The wind got up and it was colder,
though wool still curded hawthorn lanes,
chaining the farms to each other.

Notes

The Sundial

p.16   Storm Awst (Welsh): August storm.
          tyddyn (W): small holding.

p.22   Dafydd is the Medieval Welsh love poet Dafydd ap Gwilym. He names several women in his poems. I have used Dyddgu's name, though there is no evidence that, although he courted her, he ever won the real Dyddgu.

p.24   Ystrad Fflûr (Strata Florida) Cardiganshire, is traditionally held to be where Dafydd is buried.

p.27   Er Côf (W): In Memoriam.

p.33   cariad (W): love, or belovéd.

Letter from a Far Country

p.46   Jac Codi Baw (Jack dig the dirt) is a local Welsh nickname for a J.C.B.

p.47   The Saddle and the Fan are peaks in the Brecon Beacons.

p.51   Taid: the North Welsh word for grandfather.

p.55   Mamgu: the South Welsh word for grandmother.
          pais (W): petticoat.

p.62   Nain: North Welsh for grandmother.

p.63   diaconydd (W): deacon.
          trysorydd (W): treasurer.

p.81   Blodeuwedd was created from the flowers of the oak, broom and meadowsweet. She was turned into an owl as a punishment for adultery. (*The Mabinogion*).

p.85   dŵr (W): water.

New poems

p.93   In a radio programme R.S. Thomas used the warm but empty form of the hare as a metaphor for the presence or absence of God.
          Legend tells that 20,000 saints are buried on the island of Enlli (Bardsey).

p.96   Castell y Bere: a castle built by Llywelyn the Last, Prince of Wales. He was killed by Edward I, his head carried on a stake to London.

Acknowledgements

Of the poems previously uncollected, some have appeared in *PN Review*, *Tenfold*, *Spectrum*, and *Ffoto Gallery*, Cardiff, to whose editors thanks are due. The author also acknowledges the Welsh Arts Council, and St David's University College, Lampeter, for the Fellowship which has enabled her to write some of the poems in this book.

The cover illustration is by Catrin Clarke.